LOVE REVEALED
Renewed Through God's Love

Alex Young, PhD

Copyright © 2021 by Alex Young, Ph.D.

All rights reserved.

All rights reserved. No part of this book may be reproduced in any manner, except for brief quotations in critical articles or reviews, without the author's written permission.

ISBN: 978-0-57882-4444 (paperback)

Cover design by 100Covers
Interior design by FormattedBooks

For my friends who encouraged me when I began to have self-doubt and felt unworthy of the task at hand, I thank and love you. I am thankful that they reminded me of God's continual love and guidance as demonstrated by Jesus Christ. My friends, you know who you are. Much love to you. I hope that this message finds those who need it and is shared with those who have lost hope. I am thankful to Holy Spirit which guided me through this process of learning about love.

Contents

Chapter 1 What Is Love?.. 1
Chapter 2 How Does Love Look in the World?................... 13
Chapter 3 Understanding God's Love....................................21
Chapter 4 How Do We Act in Love?...................................... 29
Chapter 5 Love In A Fallen World 37
Chapter 6 Conclusion 47

Notes 63
About Alex Young 65

Chapter One
What Is Love?

WHAT IS LOVE? Love has been written by many, and understood by few. As I reflect on the concept of love, I know I am still learning about it. It is an ongoing process of which pain has blocked me from experiencing. Of course, I thought love was just a feeling of caring and affection. I thought that someone could love even though they had no integrity or respect towards you. Rather, I saw this as only a character flaw in them and did not necessarily take it personally as them being unloving. I saw their actions as independent of love and representative of their upbringing. However, I have learned that a person's evil and unkind actions, is only reflective of their character; and this does not equate to love. I thought that in time that their actions would line up with what they were telling me. But, I failed to realize that their actions were only a reflection of their heart.

For the heart can only be changed by the Holy Spirit. Only God can provide and lead us toward an inclination and deep desire for His will; for God is Love. Therefore, one whose actions and speech are inconsistent with God's way is not love. The love of God is consistent and stable; human love is fickle and ever-changing.

So, about Love, what is it? Is it just caring and affection? What is affection? Is this really what love is? It seems that we think we know the answer to the question of love. However, many people struggle with the emptiness that they feel inside because love is exactly what they are searching and longing for. If we truly know what love is, why is love so hard to find? Do we really understand the meaning of love, and how it looks? Many times, we think that money, marriage, children, a big house, winning the lottery, and giving family members material possessions are indications of love. This is only a limited view of love. Love is an action, which does not just involve material goods, affectionate, or pleasurable feelings; but it also involves truth, integrity, chastisement, courage, honesty, and obedience to the will of God.

Although, I have served in mental health for many years, I am still learning about love. I find this subject of love difficult to write about. I am not a Bible scholar, I only know what has been given to me to share. But, what I have learned is that there is an invisible thread of needing love that we humans desire and need. What I have also found, is that the root of many psychological problems is found at the **heart of the matter**. Let me explain, many people who experience a deep sense of depression or anxiety are moved or triggered by emotional factors. Some of these emotional factors include feelings of anger, inadequacy, disconnection, fear, and rejection. These are residual emotions that manifest from a lack of love—this is the heart of the matter. Sometimes traumatic things happen during childhood; and some occur during adulthood. But emotions are not always fueled by what someone else actually did to them; sometimes emotions are triggered by a mistake or regret or guilt of our own doing.

For example, a person has regret about pursuing his dream and leaving his full-time job. He opted instead to work part-time while pursuing a full-time lucrative business. However, it does not work out as well as he thought for his family, and financial woes occur. Now, at face value, he is, of course, obviously upset about his finances and his inability to pay the mortgage, car note, and other major expenses. But during the session, the man reveals that he is really concerned about his wife leaving him, his children seeing him as inadequate and viewing him as less than a man, and thereby rejecting him. In his mind, he feels unlovable. When he is no longer able to sustain provision, he believes he is unworthy of love. This translates as the removal of love. He believes that he is now unlovable because of the loss of his employment. For him, his expression of love was the provision, and without him being able to provide, he felt "unlovable." Now, it may have taken several sessions to get to that point, but the heart (core) of the matter was his concern for the loss of "love." I provided this example because love for him, was based on contingencies. So when things in his situation changed, he become afraid that he would lose love. He did not realize, that he unconsciously believed that he was paying for love. That's right, *paying for love.*

Whether we realize it or not, many of us fall into the unconscious belief of *paying for love.* Yes, I said it, paying for love! Some believe unconsciously or consciously that they can make someone love them by their actions. Some use sex as currency to get what they believe is love from another person. However, sex and attractiveness does not equate to love. Or some may believe that attractiveness or wealth will bring them love. However, this is all vanity and temporary, for when these things are gone; to them, they believe they are unlovable or unworthy of love.

This fallacy has caused many to consider suicide, lead to suicides, unhealthy behaviors, depression, and chronic anxiety because they are believing in the world's standards of love. This is not love, God is Love. Love has been illustrated throughout the Bible, and the actions are represented through the sacrifice of God's Son, Jesus Christ, and by Jesus' examples of love throughout His time on earth. Even during that time, people missed the point, and Jesus was persecuted anyway. The world was infiltrated with tradition, pride, and ambition. The purity of the heart was revealed by actions, and the ultimate reflection of God's Love, was Jesus, God with us.

Love. The definition of love according to the Merriam-Webster online dictionary is as follows: Love- Noun 1) a)strong affection for another arising out of kinship or personal ties; b) attraction based on sexual desire: affection and tenderness felt by lovers; c) Affection based on admiration, benevolence, or common interests. Verb: 1) feel a deep romantic or sexual attachment to someone; 2) a warm attachment, enthusiasm, or devotion; 3) a: the object of attachment, devotion, or admiration; b: a beloved person; and Verb: 1) to hold dear (cherish); b: to feel a lover's passion, devotion, or tenderness for. According to Webster's Dictionary (2000), Love defined as a Noun: 1) Strong affection; 2) warm attachment; 3: beloved person; and defined as verb as 1) feel affection for; and 2) enjoy greatly. Notice that definition only scratched the surface of love, it is shallow at best.

Why this word is used so much, but not understood fully? Sometimes, when love is presented as pure, it is not well received, because love has been misused throughout time. It is not truly represented in the lives of many people who experience love in the human worldly sense. They have a limited understanding or perception of love, because human capacity is limited. It is limited within the flesh in and of itself. Love manifest its true presence when the Holy Spirit is made manifest within the heart of person. This occurs when the voice of the Holy Spirit is predominant in that person's life and the life s/he chooses to walk accordingly in obedience and humility.

Love is complicated by the world's standards. In that the way that the world defines love contradicts *how we as humans genuinely want to experience love.* Yes, Love is a verb, but worldly love is a verb in the sense that something has is done to prove our love to another or to be worthy of love? Is (love) a product of keeping tabs on who is receiving and giving "The most?" Wherein, when s/he who gives the most, is the one that most loves you or that s/he that gives the least is the one loves the least? Is love based on quantity, quality, or neither? Is this relevant to the concept of Godly Love? We will examine this further.

But first, let us look at how love is generally viewed. Based on the secular (worldly) view, or Webster's dictionary, love is a feeling. Well, here is the problem with feelings, feelings change, and feelings are fickle, not dependable, and easily subjective to the temperament of the person or the situation. Love in this sense is based on the person experiencing a feeling, which could very well run into the concept of having a reason to love you. And if there is a reason, is it really love? So here's the problem with that, what happens when the reason for loving you goes away, as a result of change over time, will you still be lovable, will that person still love you: These are hard questions, I know, but it is something that we have to think about. Is God's love for us based on our actions or something superficial about us? Here are several statements below:

-Love is a feeling   True or False
-Love has a reason   True or False
-Love is contingent   True or False
-Love is prideful   True or False
-Love is protective   True or False
-Love is fearless   True or False

According to God's word, we, humans are not worthy of God's Love, but he loved us anyway. God gave His only Son, Jesus. God so loved the world that He gave his only begotten Son, so that we may have life. However, there was no reason, because we were not worthy and we (humans) were not deserving of the sacrifice. But yet God loves us and desires salvation for us. God's love is demonstrated by his grace when we are unlovable. God's love is demonstrated by his longsuffering even when we are slow to change. God's love is even present when we do not love ourselves and when we:

Do not know how to love ourselves;
Do not care for our bodies (temples; abuse our bodies);
Do not understand love;
Do not acknowledge God's presence.

In 2 Peter 3:9 (KJV) - *"The Lord is not slack concerning his promise, as some men count slackness; but is longsuffering to us-ward, not willing that any should perish, but that all should come to repentance."* This indicates that God's longsuffering is for our good, this is a demonstration of His love for us. See, 2 Peter 3: 15 (KJV), *"And account that the longsuffering of our Lord is salvation; even as our beloved brother Paul also according to the wisdom given unto him hath written unto you;"* God waits for us to change because He wants the best, He wants us saved because he loves us.

The concept of love, as I learned in the world, pushed me into some aversive and abusive situations. I was searching for love outside of myself, outside of God. Because I lacked the true understanding and knowledge of what love was, I was vulnerable to the deception of love. I thought it was measured by how much the person gives, in the form of time, money, or goods. I did not examine the heart. The heart is the source to identify the true motive- to identify if love is the true reason for the action. The heart reveals that person's true motivation. The motivation behind actions is a key determinant as to whether true love is in the picture; or whether that person is using you to just to fill a void or gain something. I was seeking fulfillment from someone or something that only God could fulfill. Seeking a feeling, an entity outside of ourselves will not fill that void. For God is Love!!

I was seeking validation outside of myself and did not know how true love looked. When someone recognizes your imperfections and still stay to hear you out; this is love. When they give you the space you need to heal, while being compassionate through the process that is love. Love is not only present when everything is rosy, but also when things are bad. Love is present through the hard times and the good times, through the in-depth talks, the ugly, and the honest to truth talks, and the misunderstandings. Love is not prideful or hurtful, it is gentle, compassionate, long-suffering, and patient. It does not rush one to make haste or meet one's selfish desires. Love is true. Therefore, to love unconditionally, which includes, freely giving, protective, and a source of energy that you would lay down your life someone, is referred to as **Agape** Love. Jesus laid down His life for us, so that we could have salvation. We will review the 4 types of love (Lewis, 1960), but the love that is most stable, consistent, and unconditional love is Agape love.

FOUR TYPES OF LOVE

- **Storge** – affectionate love through familiarity (also is a matter of reason), for example- "I love you because you are my mother" or "Love you because you are my child"

- **Philia** – Friendship love, a strong platonic connection between individuals (It's a reason for this love, not unconditional)
- **Eros** – Sexual, Lustful, romantic feelings of "love" (being in love)—an emotional feeling of love
- **Agape** – Unconditional Love (God Love- sacrificial love)

In mankind, there seems to be limited "true love."-True love is often misrepresented as in "I love you because", based on contingency. For clarity, unconditional love will be referred to as true love. Love is not contingent on acting or behaving a certain way. When there is change, we humans remind you constantly of your past mistakes, while avoiding our own shortcomings. We tend to pass judgment without thought and condemn others when they are at their lowest. This is not from God.

Humans use avoidance, distraction, and flat out lies to avoid being forthcoming, which is a means of self-deceived protection against their own heart. But look, what is happening, is a spiritual heart condition where they harden their own hearts, guard themselves against receiving new love, learning the truth, or bearing the truth. No human is perfect, but only with God, can they go through the process daily, denying their egos, denying their own desires, while walking in obedience.

The following verses describe the God's commandment of love:

> "*A new commandment I give unto you, That ye love one another; as I have loved you, that ye also love one*

another. By this shall all men know that ye are my disciples, if ye have love to one another." John 13:34-35 (KJV)

"And now abide in faith, hope, love, these three; but the greatest of these is love." I Corinthians 13:13 (NKJV)

"In this the children of God are manifest, and the children of the devil: whosoever doeth not righteousness is not of God, neither he that loveth not his brother. For this is the message that ye heard from the beginning, that we should love one another." I John 3:10-11 (KJV)

"Beloved, let us love one another, for love is of God; and everyone who loves is born of God and knows God. He who does not love does not know God, for God is love. In this the love of God was manifested toward us, that God has sent His only begotten Son into the world, that we might live through Him. In this is love, not that we loved God, but that He loved us and sent His Son to be the propitiation for our sins. Beloved, if God so loved us, we also ought to love one another. No one has seen God at any time. If we love one another, God abides in us, and His love has been perfected in us." I John 4:7-12 (NKJV)

You see, the above scriptures tell the commandment of love. They explain the importance of love; describes the way love looks and behaves. There is no grey area; we either love or hate. For it is noted in I John 7-12, that God gave his only Son, Jesus Christ for the atonement of our Sins.

CHAPTER TWO

HOW DOES LOVE LOOK IN THE WORLD?

FOR SOME, LOVE means protection and security. But yet, still at times, there are contingencies. In the human scope and the world, "Love" as in the "word" has been used to describe many feelings and actions which are not indeed (love). At times, it is represented (acted) as an obsession, overbearing, overprotection, controlling, and feared (which is by the the way, not respected). Even in the negative action, such as physical aggression, it is seen by some as love; but any reasonable person would say that this is not loving. It may be hard to decipher what is love when all you know, as the victim, is hearing the abuser repeatedly say the phrase, "I love you", while being abused. The abusers explain their behaviors as acts of love. For example, the abuser say, "This is the reason why I hit you in mouth is because I wanted to correct before you made a fool of yourself." They may justify their actions by blaming the victim for their behaviors. Sometimes the individuals mistake those behaviors as love; and believe that those aggressive assaults are love. This is not love. You see, what we sometimes sincerely believe is love, is actually not.

"The heart is deceitful above all things, and desperately wicked: who can know it?" Jeremiah 17: 9 (KJV). Sometimes our own heart deceives us, and we believe that we are loved. We believe that we are loving, because we are still perceiving love as a feeling. It is amazing how sometimes we cannot feel love when there is love all around us. And I say this, because people may say that they love you, but it does not reflect in their actions, expressions, or motives. Which makes come to question of knowing or recognizing what love is while in experiencing pain.

Is it possible to receive love if you have not healed? Are you not whole, if you are not healed? Can you have a "loving partner" and not be fully healed? Do we have to be perfect in the sense of being fully healed, to have others to love us, or show us, love? Can part of this emptiness come from a lack of understanding and perception? Can our pain and experiences, distort our reality and our perception of love. Healing comes through God, and the more we get know God, the more we can understand and forgive ourselves. The issue of pain and love will discussed in more detail later. But, first let us look at how God loves us in the following passage and how we should love:

> *"Hereby perceive we the love of God, because he laid down his life for us: and we ought to lay down our lives for the brethren. But whoso hath this world's good, and seeth his brother have need, and shutteth up his bowels of compassion from him, how dwelleth the love of God in him? My*

little children, lets us not love in word, neither in tongue; but in deed and truth." 1 John 3:16-18 (KJV)

Reflections

I was showing love to others, through constant giving and serving, genuinely believing that my acts were coming from a pure place, but they were coming from a place of "longing to be loved" and "not wanting to be rejected." Someone once told me and began to believe this for the very first time, that "You don't have to do anything but be you, you are good the way that you are." I did not realize how much I was longing for someone to love, anyone, especially a male. I thought that I needed a husband to be fulfilled, but God showed and told me that I all needed was Him and that his love was ever-present. Follow after Me, MY child, and I will give you the desires of your heart. See Psalm 37:4 (KJV) – *"Delight thyself also in the Lord; and he shall give you the desires of thine heart."* I did not know that the true depth of pain was that I was not fully healed and that all my longing was for love, has to do with what I had lost, and what I had been warring against all my life.

This life which I have spoken to God as a child, asking Him, "Why did he put me in this place?" Apparently, I had some inkling that my purpose was divine and special, but I was not prepared for the warfare that I would face throughout my life. But, my God was and is ever faithful and intervened in my ignorance and immaturity- I experienced His love. The Lord was my help and protection!!! This passage reflects God's love- *"Fear thou not; for I am with thee: be not dismayed; for I am thy God: I will strengthen thee; yea, I will help thee; yea, I will uphold thee with the right hand of my righteousness."* Isaiah 41:10 (KJV)

We cannot understand the love of God until we have starting walking daily in a relationship with Jesus Christ; so that we can walk in the fullness of what God destined for our life. God's love is the only love that we should expect as unconditional and unchanging. For God's word is not void and does not change. But living in the world, being human, sometimes makes it hard to remember that. For the love of others, for it is not good for man to be alone (when God made Eve for Adam); and that two is better than one. Yes, we are social beings and we desire and need love; but we must not chase after love in man. We must always trust and put God first. *"Delight thyself also in the Lord; and he shall give thee the desires of thine heart."* Psalm 37:4 (KJV)

Even though we have running water, lights, food in the refrigerator, we seemed to forget or not understand that this is God's love and grace for us. This is one of the many ways that God is showing His love. Therefore, it is important that we do not venture into the realm of "ungratefulness." Are we not grateful when we become saddened over an ending (which may very well be the beginning)? Sometimes, an ending relationship (which in the ego, the human mind sees as failure) feels like rejection; although the rejection did not begin or end with that relationship, but begin with that person. Sometimes, by our worldly standards, we feel rejected and unloved when others fail to perform according to our expectations. For example, when she or he fails to give a birthday present, Valentine's gift, or even a Christmas gift- but what does all this means- we sometimes feel unloved. Are we expecting a form of expression of love, and missing what the person is showing you? The person may express love differently from what you are expecting.

Sometimes our expectations of other people lead us into disappointment and despair, over the question; does the person really cares about me or the does the person really loves me?" You see those are all those thoughts that we form are sometimes based on how we were taught through experience. It is a hard lesson to unlearn those ways of thinking. It can be painful and seem unreal, but passing the lesson is part of your healing toward forgiveness, to allow you to receive love. But we are greater than we think we are because God formed us. God is love and God formed you, for He knew you before you were formed. Because we are taught to measure love by how much someone does or spends on us…this is an unfortunate fallacy. The amount (quantity) that a person gives you, does not necessarily mean that this is love. For love is a measure of the heart, and out of the heart comes the truth of the motive. *"Keep thy heart with all diligence; for out of it are the issues of life." Proverbs 4:23 (KJV)*

On many reality shows, you may find that there is a woman married to a wealthy man, who gives her everything, and she is a careless spender, spending as if the money will be there forever—she shows no virtue in her movements, plans, or provisions for others. Then all of sudden she decides she is tired of the abuse and/or he decides he wants a younger woman, he cuts her off financially, and now she feels her life has ended. Because all the people that she thought "loved" her have abandoned her; she realized that her money and status were only keeping them around. So the point here, is that wealth and material goods do not equate to love. This is not a requirement of true love.

In another case, this was a young lady dating this guy who would always take her on expensive dates and buy her expensive gifts, but she was unaware of his motive of being after what she had or his plans of murder after he got a life insurance policy on her. She initially thought that he "loved" her because of his actions. She also thought that sex could keep him interested, but sexual attraction does not equate to love and does not make another person love you.

Someone once told me, "Don't expect anything, that way you won't be disappointed." After a time, I began to understand that, as my mind has persistently failed me, and caused my emotions to go array; and get carried away with what I thought the outcome should have been or what the person should have done for me. I became entitled and like a spoiled child, whose emotions changed because, "I did not get what I wanted", or "I did not get what I expected." This in the end, was only self-inflicted pain, emotional pain that dims the light that God was shining on my life. I was thinking about how I had been disappointed because I did not get something that I wanted. I looked and wondered why I am feeling sorry for myself and why I am troubled. When God has already worked things out, I only needed to take my hands and my "mouth off of it" (keep silent about the situation—observe in prayer). Specifically, I needed to release my problem to Lord, in the name of Jesus, for He loves me. I realize that I was trying to get from humanity, something that only God could provide.

CHAPTER THREE

UNDERSTANDING GOD'S LOVE

O N LOVING GOD and Others. If we understand how God loves, and how much He loves us, it would be easier for people to love others. Because no one is perfect, no action is perfect, the person always will have consequences whether good or bad. However, we as humans are not good all the time, many do not acknowledge God's existence or act in the way of righteousness, though confessing to being of God (i.e., Christian). Even so, the Lord continues to extend love and grace amid our evil deeds, missteps, and **ignor(e)-ance** of Him. We ignore God by not spending time with Him, by not studying the word, by not acknowledging His presence in all that we do, by not trusting; by not listening. We think we have knowledge of Him, but we have no knowledge of him. We have become ignorant of God. Therefore, we must love God, because He first loved us. To do this, we must follow His way. Our love is demonstrated through obedience and the surrender of our life to God.

> *"And thou shalt love the Lord thy God with all thy heart, and with all thy soul, and with all thy mind, and with all thy strength: this is the first commandment. And the second is like, namely this, Thou shalt love thy neighbor as thyself. There is none other commandant greater than these."* Mark 12:30-31 (KJV)

For God so loved the World, That he gave his only begotten son, Jesus, for the salvation of the world, Love is our birthright, is has been given to us by God and through the blood of Jesus. *"Beloved, let us love one another: for love is of God; and every one that loveth is born of God, and knoweth God. He that loveth not knoweth not God; for God is love. In this was manifested the love of God toward us, because that God sent his only begotten Son into the world, that we might live through him. Herein is love, not that we loved God, but that he loved us, and sent his Son to be the propitiation for our sins. Beloved, if God so loved us, we ought also to love one another. No man hath seen God at any time. If we love one another, God dwelleth in us, and his love is perfected in us."* 1 John 4:7-12 KJV

The love of God is a gift and His sacrifice for people. This is the love of God, Agape Love- an unconditional love and love without reason. At the time of receipt, is foreign and difficult to comprehend this type of love in a fallen world. It is difficult because the worldly love is based on, contingencies, greed, self-centeredness, instant gratification, lust, and evil warring against humankind. When we give authority to such evil spirits, either intentionally or unintentionally, we lack the understanding of the power that worked within us, because of being dulled to Love and sharpen with evil. There is lack of understanding that we have the power to manifest a change in our own mind and bodies to create a presence of love in our own selves, true love, in their own selves through the power of the Holy Spirit. The power of Love, is untouched, for God is Love.

In *I John 3:16-18 (KJV)*, "*Hereby perceive we the love of God, because he laid down his life for us: and we ought to lay down our lives for the brethren. But whoso hath this world's good, and seeth his brother in have need, and shutteth up his bowels of compassion from him, how dwelleth the love of God in him? My little children, let us not love in word, neither in tongue; but in deed and in truth.*" For if a person does not know God, s/he does not know God, for God is love. "*Behold what manner of love the Father has bestowed on us, that we should be called the children of God! Therefore the world does not know us, because it did not know Him.*" 1 John 3:1 (NKJV). This is also further discussed in the scripture below:

> "*Whosoever shall confess that Jesus is the Son of God, God dwelleth in him, and he in God. And we have known and believed the love that God hath to us. God is love; and he that dwelleth in love dwelleth in God, and*

God in him. Herein is our love made perfect, that we may have boldness in the day of judgment: because as he is, so are we in this world. There is no fear in love; but perfect love casteth out fear: because fear hath torment. He that feareth is not made perfect in love. We love him, because he first loved us. If a man say, I love God, and hateth his brother, he is a liar: for he that loveth not his brother whom he hath seen, how can he love God whom he hath not seen? And this commandment have we from him, That he who loveth God love his brother also."
1 John 4:15-21 (KJV)

Can someone in pain give Love? Can someone in pain receive love? Are you in pain today? Do you know the origin of your pain?

Uncovered Pain. Sometimes people experience several stressful and unfortunate events. This is the human condition (see reference Adam & Eve, see Genesis 3). Some things we have control over; and some are, of which, we have no control over or responsibility. These events can cause pain in individuals. These events can be caused by one person, several persons, or by a series of causes unrelated to human factors. In the short of it all, it has left the individual with a scar, unseen and unacknowledged to others, and hidden by the person who is in pain. Thus, the subject of pain is covered for several reasons—Pain can lead to: 1) a living death; 2) a lack of fullness in life, which affects work, relationships, mental and physical well-being; and, 3) holding onto something that gives very little value to life, a factor of control that we refuse to let go of, our sense of control. So we believe, it is our safety net to not talk about the pain, it is the safe haven. For there is a refusal to surrender the deception of power, the power that we think we have to cover the pain.

For pain to be covered, it is masked, it is bandaged and cannot be healed. Therefore, what is to come of the individual? How must the pain be uncovered? Do we have the courage to do so, only God can uncover the pain (only God can deliver)…even if we do not know the origin or want to acknowledge the pain. The uncovering, unveiling of your pain is your testimony to God's unconditional Love and Grace. God is holding, and God wants to hold you, to cradle you, if only you will surrender. Surrender to the unveiling of God's Glory for your life!

Why did I talk about pain? Because this could be the very thing that hinders you from love, from receiving love and from giving love. Sometimes when we are in pain, our actions look like love, because we are constantly giving, providing, and nurturing others in order to secure love in some way. In our own way we think if we act *good*; that person will like us, then the love will be given. We believe that somehow we will not encounter pain, "In that situation as long as I go along with the plan" mindset. So we drift into a *people-pleasing* mode and lose ourselves until there is nothing left. So when the person leaves us (i.e., end of relationship, death, sickness), we go into a depression, because that person has become our whole world. We had invested so much "love" in this person that once they are gone, we think, "There is no more love to give or receive," and we believe, "I am unlovable." This can be very dangerous because it sometimes spirals a person into suicidal thoughts. After all, they began to believe the lies of the enemy, the lies of this world. They believe that the source of love is in the world and of the world. How did I get here? How do we get here? How do we prevent this from happening?

The Source of Love is from God. Let me repeat, the source of true love is always from God. God made and formed us. We are from God. Love is there within us, this is why we long for it, whether we know it or not. If many of us really understood this, despite our circumstances, we would have more joy and give love more genuinely. How many of us are willing to give sacrificial love for her/his brother? I for sure, know that is not the natural inclination of humans unless in some cases, it applies to offspring. For if asked, it gives us pause to do so.

When I think about the love that God has for us, we, who are so undeserving, my heart pauses with overwhelm. The fact that God gave Jesus Christ to die for our sins so that we may have salvation. God gave us Jesus Christ, ***Immanuel***, God with Us. This absolutely takes my breath away and it is mind-blowing to understand the sacrifice and the effects of generations of people in the world. From this, God has given us a gift through Jesus Christ. For in ***Ephesians 1: 4-6 (KJV)***, *"According as He hath chosen us in Him before the foundation of the world, that we should be holy* *and without blame before him in love: Having predestined us unto the adoption of children by Jesus Christ to himself, according to the good pleasure of his will, To the praise of the glory of his grace, wherein he hath made us accepted in the beloved."*

CHAPTER FOUR

HOW DO WE ACT IN LOVE?

How does love look? In scripture, Jesus Christ was the ultimate example of love through his many encounters. Jesus is constant, renewing, uplifting, and never changing. Jesus' earth walk was meant to teach us about how to love. For love, was the commandment that was held above all other laws, gifts, and sacrifices? This is what 1 Corinthians 13: 1-13 (NKJV), tells us about love:

> *"Though I speak with the tongues of men and of angels, but have not love, I have become sounding brass or a clanging cymbal. And though I have the gift of prophecy, and understand all mysteries and all knowledge, and though I have all faith, so that I could remove mountains, but have not love, I am nothing. And though I bestow all my goods to feed the poor, and though I give my body to be burned, but have not love, it profits me*

nothing. Love suffers long and is kind; love does not envy; love does not parade itself, is not puffed up; does not behave rudely, does not seek its own, is not provoked, thinks no evil; does not rejoice in iniquity, but rejoices in the truth; bears all things, believes all things, hopes all things, endures all things. Love never fails. But whether there are prophecies, they will fail; whether there are tongues, they will cease; whether there is knowledge, it will vanish away. For we know in part and we prophesy in part. But when that which is perfect has come, then that which is in part will be done away. When I was a child, I spoke as a child, I understood as a child, I thought as a child; but when I became a man, I put away childish things. For now we see in a mirror, dimly, but then face to face. Now I know in part, but then I shall know just as I also am known. And now abide faith, hope, love, these three; but the greatest of these is love."

We must show love when another person is in need, we must care for the fatherless and widows, but must not turn away the sick, broken-hearted, and the crippled. We must esteem each human, man, child, or woman with the love and grace that Jesus showed. For God gives us new mercies daily- each day is new, we can only go forward, not backward. For we have not the power to change the past, we can only focus on the "here and now."

It takes practice to move in love. To begin to move in love, we must gain knowledge, understanding, and wisdom of application.

We must know the time and the season for which we are to move in that way. See Ecclesiastes 3:1, 8 (KJV) – "*To everything there is a season, and a time to every purpose under the heaven:*" *v.8 "A time to love, and a time to hate; a time of war, and a time of peace."*

Moving in love, implies action, a motion, an act. Love is shown by the person's way of life. It does not appear arbitrarily because it comes from the matter of the heart. The heart is the factor that propels the person to move in love. The issue of charity (i.e., aka love), is one that is demonstrated in many ways and means different things to the person receiving it. Let me explain, Love, is a heart condition. The heart is the indicator of the source of the movement. The heart propels motive and motive guides movement. Therefore the actions of individuals can reveal the motive. For in *John 13: 34-35 (KJV)*: "*A new commandment I give unto you, That ye love one another; as I have loved you, that ye also love one another. By this shall all men know that ye are my disciples, if ye have love one to another.*" Discussed below, there are several actions that are valuable in growth.

Moving in Love involves the Discipline of the Tongue. Action, you should know that words should be seasoned and when to speak and when not to speak. Your words would be used for edification and not for tearing down. For one's speech is an illustration of one's heart condition. "Keep thy heart with all diligence; for out of it are the issues of life." *(Proverbs 4:23, KJV)*. Also in *Colossians 4:6 (NKJV),* "Let your speech always be with grace, seasoned with salt, that you may know how you ought to answer each one." Also, keeping control of what you say, helps to preserve both you and your relationships. "Whoso keepeth his mouth and his tongue keepeth his soul from troubles."(*Proverbs 21:23 KJV*). For I was listening to a sermon, and the speaker stated, "Love is expressed through communication, and without communication, there is no love." (Grace Digital, March 2020). What we say can either destroy or uplift a person. *"Death and life are in the power of the tongue: and they that love it shall eat the fruit thereof."* Proverbs 18:21 (KJV)

Moving in Love involves Forgiveness. God has forgiven our sins, from the moment we ask, we are forgiven. Each day is made new. In this, God even gives us grace in the mistakes and missteps of disobedience, and the consequences thereafter. For there are consequences, even when we are forgiven.

Moving in Love involves Longsuffering. The mercy that God shows us daily is the mercy that we should show to one another. Love is patient, Love is not grudging, love is not controlling. God with all His power, is not controlling but gives us free will. This is why we must learn to hear God's voice clearly, by dying to our voice daily, to hear and gain the mystery of love in action. In *Proverbs 16:9 (KJV)*, *"A man's heart devised his way: but the Lord directeth his steps."*

Moving in Love involves Compassion. If someone is in need, we should have the compassion to move in action, not just in word, saying, "I will pray for you." But we should be moved to emphasize and hear during their time of trouble. It is important that we show our love, by being kind and compassionate toward one another. In *Ephesians 4:32* (NKJV), *"And be kind to one* *another, tenderhearted, forgiving one another, even as God in Christ forgave you."*

Moving in Love involves Grace. Understanding the unmerited and abounding love of God. What is grace- it is unmerited divine assistance, according to Webster's Dictionary. We are to love that way, because God loves us. *"Beloved, if God so loved us, we also ought to love one another. No one has seen God at any time. If we love one another, God abides in us, and His love has been perfected in us." I John 4:11-12 (NKJV).*

"For by grace are ye saved through faith; and that not of yourselves: it is the gift of God: Not of works, lest any man should boast." Ephesians 2:8-9 (KJV).

Moving in Love with Knowledge & Wisdom. Knowledge and Wisdom without love and compassion can make us miss the target. We may have the knowledge, but not have the wisdom in how to move correctly. So you ask, if I have the knowledge and wisdom, why I need Love. You need love because correction has to come from a pure place, love. And remember, God is love. This must be the motivation by which we are to move. It is only through the love of God, that truth and purpose can be revealed. We must season our words during periods of correction so that we have done our part in the plan. *"Death and life are in the power of the tongue: and they that love shall eat the fruit thereof." (Proverbs 18:21 KJV)*

At times, it seems no matter how you "season your words" and how pure your act of love is, some may continue to carry the offense when love and forgiveness are absent in their own hearts. In that case, you have done your part, sometimes people are not ready to receive the message, and at times will reject the gift of the message. But do not be discouraged. For further reference on wisdom, turn your attention to Proverbs, a book of wisdom in the Bible.

The following scriptures express the above passage more clearly while emphasizing the importance and the commandment of love. It shows how all other gifts and actions are deemed as null and void if there is no love. Once again, I remind you, it's a matter of the heart. The matter of the heart is the **heart posture** or the motivation for the actions. The quality and quantity are not as relevant as the heart posture.

"Though I speak with tongues of men and of angels, and have not charity, I am become as a sounding brass, or a tinkling cymbal. And though I have the gift of prophecy, and understand all mysteries, and all knowledge; and though I have all faith, so that I could remove mountains, and have not charity, I am nothing. And though I bestow all my goods to feed the poor, and though I give my body to be burned, and have not charity, it profiteth me nothing. Charity suffered long, and is kind; charity envieth not; charity vaunteth not itself, is not puffed up,
" I Corinthians 13:1-4 (KJV)

Therefore, it imperative that we learn to trust God. But to do that, we must be able to hear God. We must train ourselves to hear, by spending time with him. "Trust in the Lord with all thine heart; and lean not unto thine own understanding." (*Proverbs 3:5 KJV*). This is where our path takes us to continue in love while living in this world.

Chapter Five
Love In A Fallen World

THE WORLD, IN the present state of things, is full of sin and is fallen. It seems that everything that is wrong, is considered right; and what is right is condemned. This is due to deception caused by the prince of this world (see Genesis 3). The beginning of this can be traced back to Adam and Eve in the Garden of Eden. God created the world and created Adam to be the overseer of all things of the earth. Eve was created from Adam's rib, hence, a woman was created as a helper unto Adam who was ruled by God, the Father. In Genesis 3, it shows how disobedience led to the fall of man.

> *"Now the serpent was more cunning than any beast of the field which the Lord God had made. And he said to the woman, "Has God indeed said, 'You shall not eat of every tree of the garden'?" And the woman said to the*

*serpent, "We may eat the fruit of the trees of the garden; but of the fruit of the tree which **is** in the midst of the garden, God has said, 'You shall not eat it, nor shall you touch it, lest you die." Then the serpent said to the woman, "You will not surely die. For God knows that in the day you eat of it your eyes will be opened, and you will be like God, knowing good and evil." Genesis 3:1-4 (NKJV)*

With this, Eve was deceived and ate from the tree, thinking that this was something good and Adam followed suit. As a result of disobedience, there were consequences for mankind. There was knowledge of good and evil, but there was disobedience of God's commandment. "*So the Lord God said to the serpent: "Because you have done this, You are cursed more than all cattle, And more than every beast of the field; On your belly you shall go, And you shall eat dust All the days of your life. And I will put enmity Between you and the woman, and between your seed and her Seed; He shall bruise your head, And you shall bruise His heel." Genesis 3:14-15 (NKJV)*

Even with all of God's consequences, He gives chastisement out of love, and with this is grace. For example, God provided a savior (the Seed that would bring forth Jesus Christ) that would conquer the serpent. Therefore, we ought not to be proud, but to walk in humility. Humility is not the same as being a doormat, but humility allows us to be grateful, to understand our position, our power source of God, our short-comings, and to remain sober (clarity of mind). With humility, love comes because there is understanding. The understanding comes from the ability to hear as result of humility (i.e., lack of pride or ego getting in the way of truth and guidance).

God's love is enough, to provide us with salvation even in the beginning when Adam and Eve both ate from the forbidden tree (tree of life). The evil in this world could be overwhelming and seductive in that we forget the purpose or miss finding/hearing the purpose that God has for us in this earth walk. Even in the beginning, there was a promise for salvation, even though it did not appear as such by human eyes. God's timing is not our own, and His ways are not like our own (*Isaiah 55:8-9, KJV*). This is why it is imperative that we stay humble so that we can hear instruction from God through the word and Holy Spirit. *"Humble yourselves therefore under the mighty hand of God, that he may exalt you in due time: Casting all your care upon him; for careth for you."* (*I Peter 5: 6-7 KJV*).

To Love correctly, as stated earlier we must have discernment and wisdom with vigilance. For in the Bible, examples of love are shown by Jesus. However, there are instructions for **what we are not to love**. Because what we love, instructs, and guides our being and our hearts. In *1 John 2:15-17*, it tells what and how we should love and why.

> *"Love not the world, neither the things that are in the world. If any man love the world, the love of the Father is not in him. For all that is in the world, the lust of the*

> *flesh, and the lust of the eyes, and the pride of life, is not of the Father, but is of the world. And the world passeth away, and the lust thereof: but he that doeth the will of God abideth forever."* 1 John 2:15-17 (KJV)

In short, the things of this world are temporary, nothing is permanent, no person is on earth forever, no person is in a position forever, people died, people retire, houses are built, houses are torn down, fashion changes daily, as with tradition, values, and cultural values, emotions are up and down, nothing is the same for long. There are seasons for all things, and beginning and an ending.

Many times we become discouraged because of the state of the world. Feeling that no matter how hard we try, it seems that evil always win. Or when you hear people, say, "When it rains it pours." This indicates that many serious distressful events have taken place in a person's life simultaneously. Sometimes, you find that individuals who are trying to be good, kind, compassionate, and honest are constantly feeling that they are coming up short; and that in coming up short, they stay in that place of crisis and distress despite their own efforts. In their own efforts, they sometimes forget to depend on God, when God is always there to help (see *Isaiah 41:10 KJV*). They began to take on feelings of helplessness, feeling that no matter what I do, nothing good comes. This leads to a feeling of hopelessness that nothing will ever get better. When this develops, their anxiety fuels depression, and they are in a constant cycle of worry and sadness in the midst of it all. So then, they began to compare themselves to others, which only deepens, the bitterness and disappointment that they already harbor. To find that those people which they are comparing themselves are doing so much better, and they are doing evil acts but live in happiness and riches. They began to think, maybe I should go that way too- since following the way of righteousness has not been rewarded. Unfortunately, this thinking could lead to a place of destruction when individuals realized that what appeared good, only deepens their sorrow and harden their hearts, they only began to see despair. However, in *Psalm 73 KJV*, David speaks to a very specific human issue:

> *"Truly God is good to Israel, even to such as are of a clean heart. But as for me, my feet were almost gone; my steps had well nigh slipped. For I was envious at the foolish, when I saw the prosperity of the wicked. For there are no bands in their death: but their strength is firm. They are not in trouble as other men; neither are they plagued like other men. Therefore pride compasseth them about as a chain; violence covereth them as a garment. Their eyes stand out with fatness: they have more than heart could wish. They are corrupt, and speak wickedly concerning oppression: they speak loftily. They set their mouth against the heavens, and their tongue walketh through the earth. Therefore his people return hither: and waters of a full cup are wrung out to them. And*

they say, How doth God Know? and is there knowledge in the most High? Behold, these are the ungodly, who prosper in the world; they increase in riches. Verily I have cleansed my heart in vain, and washed my hands in innocency. For all the day long have I been plagued, and chastened every morning. If I say, I will speak thus; behold, I should offend against the generation of thy children." Psalm 73:1-15 (KJV)

Once David stopped himself in thinking, and turned to God for comfort, the truth was revealed of the undoing. When comparing, the thought is that it is better 'over there.' And that the situation would eventually change, but all is temporal. Their acts of evil will not go unrewarded. And see the remainder of *Psalm 73: 16-28(KJV)*:

"When I thought to know this, it was too painful for me; Until I went into the sanctuary of God; then understood I their end. Surely thou didst set them in slippery places: thou castedst them down into destruction. How are they brought into desolation, as in a moment! they are utterly consumed with terrors. As a dream when one awaketh; so, O Lord, when thou awakest, thou shalt despise their image. Thus my heart was grieved, and I was pricked in my reins. So foolish was I, and ignorant: I was as a beast before thee. Nevertheless I am continually with thee: thou hast holden me by my right hand. Thou shalt

guide me with thy counsel, and afterward receive me to glory. Whom have I in heaven but thee? and there is none upon earth that I desire beside thee. My flesh and my heart faileth: but God is the strength of my heart, and my portion forever. For, lo, they that are far from thee shall perish: thou hast destroyed all them that go a whoring from thee. But it is good for me to draw near to God: I have put my trust in the Lord God, that I may declare all thy works." (Psalm 73:1-28 KJV)

We must continually trust in the Lord, for He always there and an ever-present spirit. In calling out his name there is power, God hears our call, He is waiting for us to surrender. God is waiting for us to acknowledge his love, for He is Love. In the above passage, it notes that God is faithful, present, and just, therefore it is good to always draw toward God at all times. When we feel unloved, this is from our flesh, this not from our spirit.

When I learned to forget myself, to deny myself, and turn to Creator, Elohim, I released my burden. For God Loved us, Jesus was sacrificed for my salvation, for our salvation—Jesus tells us to place our burdens on him, for his load is light. For Jesus said, *"Come to Me, all you who labor and are heavy laden, and I will give you rest. Take My yoke upon you and learn from Me, for I am gentle and lowly in heart, and you will find rest for your souls. For My yoke is easy and My burden is light."* Matthew 11:28-30 (NKJV)

Do not grow weary in well-doing, for we will be rewarded in the due season. Many times in life, it seems that things become tougher, the longer that we are striving. However, in the Bible, it encourages us to continue steadfast in doing good. *"And let us not grow weary while doing good, for in due season we shall reap if we do not lose heart." Galatians 6:9 (NKJV).*

Many times we want to give up on love, when we have been heart-brokened, lost, abandoned, and abused. Those things can make the journey of life difficult to seemingly bare at times, but we are reminded through faith that we have a comforter (Holy Spirit) to turn to; because God has already given the gift, we just needed to accept that gift. In life, sometimes when bad things happen to us, we began to believe the lies that they produce. We then look for ways to fill that emptiness. And when no comfort is found in the world, after many things have been tried, the individual may turn against themselves. They may turn against themselves by isolating from others, decreasing their activities, persistently worry about the situation, and fall into a place of hopelessness and helplessness. This describes the concept of depression. And sometimes this depression could lead to suicide. But even then, the power to overcome that involves surrender, surrendering to God regarding all things.

At times, we face periods of isolation through our own doing or not through our own doing; at times this isolation could feel like a punishment, and sometimes this isolation could feel like persecution. Isolation, meaning the separation or seclusion from others. Sometimes, this isolation involves a period of growth and enlightenment. At these times, God is wanting you to draw close to Him, to hear Him, and spend time with Him. Isolation can be bad in excess, but in moderation can become useful means of renewal and connection to God.

Chapter Six
Conclusion

STAYING IN THE **Race.** This is God's battle. This is not our battle, our position is to walk in faith and obedience. In *Exodus 14:14 (KJV)*, *"The Lord shall fight for you, and ye shall hold your peace."* We also need to understand the purpose that God has for us on this earth and that He has our back if we trust Him. When you do not understand your purpose or your assignment on this earth walk, you can be pulled in many different directions. Here is where the confusion starts, or ends up in a place where you never were supposed to be.

I remember when I was working on something important to me, something that I felt or thought I was supposed to do. At those times, I found myself getting side-tracked a whole lot. All of sudden, I had different opportunities coming toward me. And guess what, they were all distractions to get me off the focus of my assignment. And it worked for a time, but the Lord brought me back into the fold. I was in the process of starting a foundation, but then I began to run into all kinds of people who had a similar ministry, which at face value looked as if I was negating the purpose of God's assignment for me. For there were attacks on my mind and on my time- it was like, individuals were coming in sheep's clothing appearing as if to help and build, but the motive was to destroy and tear down. These were all distractions that delayed my outcomes for some time. However, God's love was gracious to pull me back into a place of working on my assignment.

Looking to God for Love. Many times, we look to others for love when we do not even love ourselves. Or because of the periods of persecution, abuse, and loneliness, we want to find another human to fill that void.

For many years, I could see myself, seeking love on the outside of myself. I wanted to be accepted, because for me that meant love. Unfortunately, this leads to people-pleasing behaviors that just left me depleted and disappointed. I was always disappointed by the person's actions and my expectations of them. I would find myself involved in situations, where I was more of the giver than the receiver, and when others tried to give to me, I would graciously refuse. Stating to them, that they didn't need to go out of their way for me or that they didn't need to do this kind of act or provide this gift for me. But wait, me on the other hand, I was always willing to give even if it caused me a loss, and if they refused, I was almost offended, thinking or saying, "My gift is not good enough" or "Why do you not want my help." I did not realize that I was manifesting what I was feeling about myself to others.

I wanted others to love me so much, that I would unconsciously, like an automatic behavior go beyond and above the call of duty to help them in their time of need. I was teaching others to take constantly from me, and giving them the idea that there was no need to help her or give to her, because "she got this or that." I was teaching people how not to value, respect, and love me. What I did not realize, was that I truly did not love myself. Let me say it again, I did not truly love myself. I was seeking others to fill that void. But only God could fill that void, that empty spot, heal that pain, and create boldness and fearlessness. It was only God, who was capable of wiping all my tears away from past hurts and disappointments. These people were reacting to how I taught them to treat me by my behaviors. An old saying goes, you teach people how to treat you.

Truthfully, without any action on your part, some people will set out to use, and devour, and destroy you in any way that they can. I am not speaking about these situations. Those people have purely evil intentions. I am talking about people who had no intention of hurting you, were basically good people, but your actions pushed them away from loving you. You almost appear needy to them, and that can become overwhelming to another person. Needy in the sense that you were willing to do or accept anything because you did not feel worthy of love. God can only fill this void, for God is only worthy! For it was written, that we should build ourselves up in the love of God. In *Jude 1:20-21 KJV*, *"But ye, beloved, building yourselves on your most holy faith, praying in the Holy Ghost, Keep yourselves in the love of God, looking for mercy of our Lord Jesus Christ unto eternal life."*

Walking in Love- Faith Walk. Walking in Love involves continually walking in charity even through troubled times. It's easy to love someone during times of peace, during times when people are lovable and situations are ideal. But what happens when that person disappoints you, are you treat them with hatred and disdain- you may not like the actions, but does that mean that you stop loving the person. Or when things do not go our way, do we become unlovable, depressed, persistent complainers about what is not right? The answer is no, absolutely, if we are to walk in love. We must be an example of Love if we call ourselves, Christians, or followers of Christ. When a parent continually shows love, with correction, to a child that is going down the wrong path, this is the **faith** walk. This is not to say, have no consequence, but chastisement should be out of love. God shows us love, despite our persistent failure, and gives us grace in our imperfections. Do we start treating that person who is lying, cheating, on drugs with hatred- No, we hate the actions but continue to love, and we allow them to go through correction and do not *enable* them to continue their destructive behaviors.

Walking in love does not mean that you become a "doormat" to people or that you become an "enabler" to inappropriate behavior. *Note:* Enabler means one that allows of one to continue in destructive behaviors towards oneself. Also see Google dictionary definition- "A person who encourages or enables negative or self-destructive behavior in another." Doormat- Defined as a submissive person who allows others to dominate them. This inappropriate behavior is not same as humility. We are not be people pleasers and walk in fear. "For God hath not given us the spirit of fear; but of power, and of love, and of a sound mind."

However, when you are walking in love, you can experience a real-life example of how one's life can be transformed while on this earth. It is by our conversation, verbal and nonverbal, that we can win souls for God. For if we are of God, we are love, and the truth is in us. Therefore we should not compromise or converse with evil. So if we continue in love, we become the victors in the situation. We are winning in love and through love.

Winning Through Love. This does not seem like a way to win. Because of course, to win, there must be a competition. And for there to be a competition, there must be competitors. I must compete. But look here, who is your competitor? Or, better to say, who is your enemy? What side are you on? Let me give you a clue. In this case, we are talking about Love, and God is Love. So anything or anyone who is against God is not of God. If we have God on our side, we can never lose…the battle has already been won. But in our own human nature, we focus on the temporal, the natural and become overwhelmed because we are striving in our own power. This, we must not do. We must not strive in our own power but rely on God for strength.

> *"For we wrestle not against flesh and blood, but against principalities, against powers, against the rulers of the darkness of this world, against spiritual wickedness in high places." Ephesians 6:12 (KJV)*

"For every one that doeth evil hateth the light, neither cometh to the light, lest his deeds should be reproved. But he that doeth truth cometh to the light, that his deeds may be made manifest, that they are wrought in God." John 3:20-21 (KJV)

Our strength and power comes from Lord, God only. *"I can do all things through Christ which strengtheneth me."*(Philippians 4:13 KJV). He will strengthen you if you ask. It is God's will that we are victors and overcomers. This is why the gift of salvation was given to us. *"For God so loved the world, that he gave his only begotten Son, that whosoever believeth in him should not perish, but have everlasting life. For God sent not his Son into the world to condemn the world; but that the world through him might be saved. He that believeth on him is not condemned; but he that believeth not is condemned already, because he hath not believed in the name of the only begotten Son of God." John 3:16-18 (KJV)*

So to say, "Winning through Love," is more powerful than it appears at face value. Love guides us in the path that we should take in fighting our battles. For example, is it wise to know that we do not fight "fire with fire" because it just creates more fire and destruction, but rather it would be wise to fight fire with water because it tames the fire and puts it out. Our world is living evidence of this concept, see all the destruction of the earth and loss of life through multiple wars and greed.

Many times when someone does something wrong, particularly children, we want to err on the side of chastisement, but chastisement only, without love, or punishment without an indication of love, is not effective. Sometimes, it is tempting to withdraw and withhold love when the "offense" is severe. In the case of talking back, or being disrespectful, we often want to punish only. Here is the time, to not only provide consequences, but also model the behavior of love and work through love. Children often imitate what they see, more so than what a parent says. However, it may be obedience that forces them to abide, through fear, the lesson of love is enduring, and enduring force throughout life. For God is Love- God is enduring, therefore love is enduring. Although, there are consequences- does God stop showing us love when we falter, when we fail, and when we repeat and turn from our former ways? Do we continue to withdraw or withhold love when children apologize sincerely, or when they fail to apologize timely, do we lower our standards to that of hatred? What is the balance of love and consequences? Here it is, there are consequences and chastisement, because of love; if there were no love, there would be no correction.

Love and Fear. We sometimes fear rejection, abandonment, shame, imperfection, and past mistakes, just to name a few. Fear of the unknown, fear of not knowing the outcome of an action, fear of success, fear of failure are some of the many anxieties that we encounter. However, this is directly opposite of love. For love empowers and convicts one into righteousness. And rightly so, since love is from God and God is love. God is omnipotent, ever powerful, bold, just, sovereign, but still longsuffering, merciful and loving. God's love has been demonstrated by his gift of His Son Jesus Christ to die upon the cross for our sins, so that we may have grace, salvation.

Why do have fear? We have fear because of sin. If there was no sin, there would be no shame, regret, envy, strife, jealousy, murder, and multitude of transgressions. We are not loving like God wants us to love if we are operating in fear.

God wants us to trust him, and fear negates this trust, it negates the faith. God wants us to be fearless because He is our strength in our weakness. God, the Lord Jesus, is our help. In *2 Timothy 1:7 (KJV)*, it reads, "For God hath not given us a spirit of fear; but of power, and of love, and of a sound mind." Three things noted here:

1) Power
2) Love
3) Sound Mind

When we become fearful to point of anxious thinking, our behaviors become erratic and we may say things we regret. We are not sober in our thinking. This is not of God. Fear and love are polar opposites, they are like oil and water, and they do not mix. For the word in *I John 4:18 (KJV)*, it plainly states this:

> "There is no fear in love; but perfect love cast out fear, because fear involves torment, But he who fears has not been made perfect in love."

God is love. God sent his Son, Jesus who died upon the cross for our sins and there God provided us with the Holy Spirit, our comforter to quell away our fears. As noted earlier, the fears that we have is anxiety. Anxiety is nothing more than fear. Throughout the Bible, God tells us that he is with us, and do not be afraid and do not worry about tomorrow. "Be anxious for nothing, but in everything by prayer and supplication, with thanksgiving, let your request be made known to God; and the peace of God, which surpasses all understanding, will guard your hearts and minds through Christ Jesus." (*Philippians 4:6-7, NKJV*).

We need to call upon him in time of fear, He will help. God is love. I repeat this point, because we are made perfect in knowing God and leaning on Him in all things; in growing closer to Jesus Christ. God's love is persistently demonstrated each time we wake and see a new day, and have an opportunity to change and work toward His perfect will for healing and redemption.

Fear stimulates stagnation and stops one from living life fully, from loving or even knowing what is your God-given assignment, whereas, love empowers, promotes, and creates. Love is the force of life that fear tries to darken and destroy. First, we must start with loving ourselves. This is not the conceited, worldly, narcissist type of feeling that I am referring to, but unconditional love to care for the temple of your body given by God.

Faith & Love. As I was writing, phrases came to me that needed to be spoken about. Faith and love were one of them. It seems that phrase, "faith and love" have been used throughout the New Testament. *"And the grace of our Lord was exceedingly abundant with faith and love which is in Christ Jesus."* I Timothy 1:14 (KJV)

How do we love, when we feel that love is not reciprocated by the people you love, the people you care about. Are we missing that their capacity to love is different than our own? I sometimes think that love, feelings of love, are deceptive in that we may believe that we love, because of the idea of something that we think we desire, is really what we do not desire. That's why we must not be guided by our feelings, but by what God tells us what love is. That we are to test the spirits, testing of the heart to understand and discern the true motives of the individuals. *"Beloved, believe not every spirit, but try the spirits whether they are of God: because many false prophets are gone out into the world."* (*I John 4:1 KJV*)

The way to know how to love, is this guidance: *"Beloved, let us love one another: for love is of God; and everyone that loveth is born of God, and knoweth God. He that loveth not, knoweth not God; for God is love."* *I John 4:7-8 (KJV)*

Propitiation of Love (of God). The meaning of Propitiation-Atonement, Reparation; Propitiation for sin – The act of atoning for sin or wrongdoing (Webster's Dictionary). We cannot speak about God's love without discussing the propitiation of sins.

And ways that God shows us, Love. God demonstrates that He loves us throughout the Bible. God illustrates and reminds us to lay our burdens down and give them to him, to cast our cares to Him. *"Casting all you care upon him; for he careth for you."* (*I Peter 5:7 KJV*) and "Come unto me, all ye that labour and are heavy laden, and I will give you rest." (*Matthew 11:28 KJV*).

We can sometimes miss love when we do not resist depression. God does not want us depressed or persistently downtrodden and weary. Of course, when there is a loss, trauma, or a crisis, there is a time for sorrow, see (*Ecclesiastes 3:1, 4 KJV*) – "To everything there is a season, and a time to every purpose under the heaven: *"A time to weep, and a time to laugh; a time to mourn, and a time to dance;"*

But giving into the feeling of depression persistently, and not fighting against it, to give full authority to the enemy, Satan, is disastrous. It makes one sink further, and further into a realm of darkness, hopelessness, and helplessness, and despair. The individual listens to the voice of loss, the voice of despair, and what they do not have, gratitude is absent. For gratitude and thankfulness has to become secondary to their grief. For the problem has, in essence, become a god and idol that has been placed before the Lord, God. Depression makes one miss the point of God's love, it makes one blame God for the imperfections of life, rather than praise God for all the blessings. Some ask, where are the blessings, when there is death and trauma? And I say, let remember the blessings of being alive to tell our story, the ability to help someone with food, shelter, water, family, or clothes; and the ability to see, hear, walk; to have people who love you; and to be able to communicate with God through prayer. These are just a few examples of blessing that we sometimes neglect to acknowledge and be thankful for. Some people may have much more, some people may have much less. But unless praise is their language, the love of God is not fully acknowledged or recognized by them; nor do they show love for God. Unless praise or thanksgiving becomes primary, depression would remain the entity in charge of your life.

In psychology, depression is defined as a feeling of sadness, hopelessness, and helplessness, --- feeling of failure, worthlessness, and physical symptoms of fatigue, changes in appetite, and changes in sleep pattern (oversleeping or extreme insomnia), excessive worry, or thoughts of death. The treatments for depression include engaging with others who are less fortunate- by volunteering- instills gratefulness; daily moderate exercise, exposure to sunshine and interaction with family and/or friend, engaging in activity that is important to the individual, and changing one's thinking. Depression consist of negative, irrational thoughts, or are distorted in a way that focuses only on the "bad" aspects of the situation. In short, many of the psychological techniques includes a shift from self to that of the outside of self. In essence, depression makes one stop loving her/his self, and this is in direct contradiction of God's commandment of love. Depression is not of God, but it is another trick of the enemy.

God's love is focused on us, and God wants us to focus on Him, and nothing else before Him, and this includes depression. For God is Love. For Jesus said, "Come unto me, all ye that labour and are heavy laden, and I will give you rest. Take my yoke upon you, and learn of me; for I am meek and lowly in heart: and ye shall find rest unto your souls. For my yoke is easy, and my burden is light." *Matthew 11: 28-30 (KJV)*

Much of what we experience in life, is trouble. However, God did not promise us a trouble-free life but did promise that he is there to help us through, see *Isaiah 41:10 (KJV)*. God is there to fight our battles and comfort us through the storm while providing his Love through blessings of life and salvation through Jesus Christ. All this is ours, if we seek it and we embrace the love of God. God is there waiting. God desires that we all have salvation. This is demonstrated by God's propitiation of our sins through His love. *"Therein is love, not that we loved God, but that He loved us, and sent his Son to be the propitiation for our sins."* (*I John 4:10 KJV*)

Overall, there are many times that the word "Love" is used, but the true essence of love and what it represents comes from God. God is Love. Jesus Christ was our example of God's love in the flesh, and it is by His example that we should live. So far I have discussed the demonstration of God's love, what love is, and how we should love one another. But how do we show God that we love Him? We show God that we love Him, through acts of obedience to his word, will, and guidance for our lives. (*John 14:23, KJV*). Obedience is more valuable than sacrifice. If sacrifice falls outside of God's will, then it is vain. We are "performing in our own power." This is not walking in relationship with God, not with the will of God. It is written of vain work, "For I never knew you." See *Matthew 7:20-23 (KJV)*. What is done unto/for God must be done in spirit and truth, not of our own will; but God's will for us. For our will is vain and if of flesh, therefore, it temporary and fleeting and fickle, inconsistent with God's will. God is stable, consistent, and unchanging. For only God, cannot lie.

For many may ask how do I know God's will for my life, how can I obey if I do not know how to hear. You have to acknowledge God daily in order to follow His will. See Proverbs 3:5-6 (NKJV), *"Trust in the Lord with all your heart, And lean not on your own understanding; In all your ways acknowledge Him, And He shall direct your paths."* You have to seek God daily through His Word (i.e., Holy Bible), through prayer, mediation, and God will show you; in all this seeking (see *Jeremiah 29:13 KJV; John 10:27 KJV*) you will learn to listen to His voice, in learning to listen to Him, there must be Trust, and Courage to walk through obedience. Remember God is Love, and without God there is no love.

FINAL THOUGHTS

In writing about love, I thought I knew how to truly love. But as I continued to learn and reflect, I began to understand how much I did not know about love. I thought some actions were motivated by love, but they were motivated by fear. My actions were motivated by fear of rejection, fear of abandonment, and fear of never being loved. Love does not move from a place of fear- love and fear are contradictory. In pure love, there is no fear. Therefore, it is imperative that healing takes place to allow one to truly love. The brokenness, oozes anxiety and anxiety is fear. How can this love be pure if it comes from place of brokenness? *"There is no fear in love; but perfect love casteth out fear; because fear hath torment. He that feareth is not made perfect in love." I John 4:18 (KJV)*

Though, I thought I was fully healed, I was still living in a place of fear, not fully understanding "I am not alone, and that God is able." I was, however, still using old habits and antidotes to protect myself from hurt; when God is my only protector and healer. Thank you Jesus. God begin to show me that my love was not pure. But that it could only be perfected in Him and through Him. For God is always there, He loves you and I more than we can imagine. In *Roman 8:38-39 (KJV)*, expresses this clearly: *"For*

I am persuaded, that neither death, nor life, nor angels, nor principalities, nor powers, nor things present, nor things to come, Nor height, nor depth, nor any other creature, shall be able to separate us from the love of God, which is in Christ Jesus our Lord."

NOTES

Lewis, CS (1960). *The Four Loves*. Geoffrey Bles Publishing

"Love." Merriam-Webster.com Dictionary, Merriam-Webster, https://www.merriam-webster.com/dictionary/love. Accessed 26 Dec. 2020.

"Love." *Webster's New Explorer Large Print Dictionary*. (2000). Federal Street Press.

Parallel Bible-KJV/AMP: Large Print. Zonderavan Publishing.

You Version (KJV/NKJV). (2008-2019), Life.Church.

Grace Ditigal, A video was uploaded, in March 2020.

The King James Version (KJV), was used primarily as point of scripture ciatation, for consistency in text. The New king James Version was use minimally, only used for clarity in explanation of the text.

Disclaimer: All written information is publish in good faith and is for educational and informational purposes only. This work is not intended to substitute professional therapeutic treatment and/or pastoral counseling. This work was written to encourage, inspire, and provide insight.

About Alex Young

Alex Young is the founder The Sérah Foundation, Inc., a nonprofit organization dedicated to outreach of abused women and children. She is a loving daughter, sister, and mother. She served as college professor which inspired her passion for teaching, mentoring, and helping individuals through the healing process. Though she currently practices as a Clinical Psychologist, she found her passion serendipitously, prior to beginning her practice. It has always been a passion within her to help, comfort, and heal others. However, her passion also has been for writing. As the author of Healing to Prosperity: Restoration through God's Way and Purpose, an inspirational account of healing with God's guidance, this serves as her debut work. As she continues learn through her walk with God, her writings are cathartic. Thus, Dr. Young was inspired to start the podcast, *Healing Conversations with Alex*, while sharing her message the testimony of God's love and guidance. For more information, go to www.dralexyoung.com to follow the author's upcoming post and podcast.

www.ingramcontent.com/pod-product-compliance
Lightning Source LLC
Chambersburg PA
CBHW022121090426
42743CB00008B/947